Living with Grief in School

Guidance for Primary School Teachers and Staff

Ann Chadwick

Published in the United Kingdom by:
Family Reading Centre Ltd
126 Sutherland Avenue, Biggin Hill
Kent TN16 3HJ

A catalogue record for this booklet
is available from the British Library

ISBN 1-898538-O1-8

Edited, designed and typeset in the UK by:
Life Skills Training Services, 163 Clifton Road
Rugby, Warwickshire CV21 3QN

PRINTED BY IMPRESSIONS PRINTING TECHNOLOGY, SEVENOAKS, KENT TN14 5HD (0732) 451181

Introduction

What can you as a teacher do to help when bereavement hits your school? Perhaps a pupil or member of staff dies - or it might be a child's friend or family member. Teachers who find themselves in this predicament often don't know where to start.

Death is a taboo subject in western society. Grief hurts, and sometimes teachers are so shocked and stunned by tragic events that it is difficult to continue with the everyday teaching role.

Children are resilient, but they are probably totally unprepared for death. A teacher can help them to face this event in their lives. Death can provide a tremendous learning opportunity. As John Donne said, 'Any man's death diminishes me.' In that diminished place parents often expect the school to know what will help both themselves and their child. Hopefully this booklet will assist you in this.

Finally, make sure ancillary staff read this booklet. Often it is the playground helper or dinner lady who first picks up the news of a death. There is much they can say and do to help.

As a result, the school can become the secure, nurturing environment the bereaved person needs, at the same time providing a golden opportunity to add to pupils' understanding.

Parents often expect the school to know what will help both themselves and their child. Hopefully this booklet will assist you in this

About the author

Ann Chadwick AIMSW, MA, JP qualified as a medical social worker in 1962. She has worked at hospitals in Bradford and Cardiff, and for four years was senior family case worker for Glamorgan Children's Department. She then spent 17 years as a senior lecturer in social work.

She has produced cassettes and videos on bereavement and has led workshops throughout the UK for many bereavement counselling agencies, including Cruse, Cot Death Association and Victim Support.

She is now a pastoral worker at St Matthew's Church, Ipswich, is a school governor and regularly counsels bereaved families in the Ipswich area.

Index

Society's attitude to death

Death is a taboo subject in Britain today. Children who are caught up in the reality of it will experience half truths, being left out or even being scolded for showing feelings. They need to be taught that giving expression to grief is both normal and healthy.

Bereavement is the biggest thing that can ever happen to a person. Grief is the price we pay for love, and expressing that pain is the best way of growing through it.

For you as a staff member to cry with a little boy who comes up to say his big sister has just died shows you really care that he is hurting. The child discovers that adults feel pain. Striving to keep a stiff upper lip puts up a barrier just when the person most needs to feel the touch of human kindness.

> Crying with a little boy who comes up to say his big sister has just died shows you really care that he is hurting

Teaching opportunities

Teaching opportunities vary with the age of the child concerned.

1. Infants

For very young children, teaching about death is best done *in context,* correcting wrong perceptions:

❏ A four-year-old dying in hospital cheerfully said: 'I know what happens when you die. Sister flushes you down the loo.' He had seen tropical fish disposed of in this way. It gave a chance to correct his perception. Four days later, he was in his coffin, but by opening up the subject he showed he was ready for some relevant facts.

> For very young children, teaching about death is best done *in context,* correcting wrong perceptions

❏ Take time in class to discuss the difference between live and dead flowers. They have a certain life span - poppies die in a day while chrysanthemums might last two weeks.

❏ It is important to acknowledge the death of a school pet - such as a guinea pig - rather than buying a replacement. This serves three purposes:

1. It provides an opportunity for change. The school can decide whether to continue keeping animals or get those that are easier to keep.

2. It validates tears, exposing children to the sadness of loss and the appearance of death. When alive, the animal was warm and active. In death, it is cold and unattractive. As with the bone from the butcher that the dog has discarded, dead things become smelly and must be disposed of. Children need to know that sadness and tears are acceptable. An important lesson is to help them accept that death hurts since it is the price we pay for love. Big boys (and girls) *do* cry!

3. It provides a chance to discuss the rites of passage of the dead. Children may well want some form of burial service for the guinea pig. This is welcome, and it can have surprisingly beneficial results!

2. Juniors

By seven, children know the difference between the concrete and the ephemeral. They can grasp the concept of 'never returning' and can see some of the social consequences of a death in a family. Sadly, families give conflicting pictures of how to view death:

> By seven, children can grasp the concept of 'never returning'

❐ An eight-year-old picks up a dead hedgehog. 'Don't touch that - it's dead,' says the parent.

❐ The parent says, 'Heaven's a happy place where Granny's at peace.' The child thinks, 'So why's everyone crying so much?'

❐ The parent explains, 'God wanted Daddy to live in heaven with him so he came and took him.' The child thinks, 'Why should God have him? I wanted Daddy to live *here* with us.'

❐ The parent says, 'We had to have the cat put to sleep.' Grandad's grave reads, 'Fallen asleep in the arms of Jesus.' The child thinks, 'I'm too scared to go to sleep in case I die like them. Anyway, what does Mummy mean when she shouts, "You children go to sleep at once!"?'

❏ Perhaps unkindest of all, and one that affects people for years to come, the parent says, 'Don't cry. You're the man of the house now that Daddy's dead.' The child thinks, 'I'm nine and I've got to look after Mummy. What's that mean - drive the car, go out to work, climb ladders, paint the house?'

Death and decay aren't subjects normally talked about, but children often want to know the answers.

Permit healthy questioning - 'Do worms come and eat you up?' - and look for chances to teach the facts of death.

Heaven or . . . ?

By its very nature, death stirs up a spiritual awareness and provides an important teaching opportunity about beliefs.

By its very nature, death stirs up a spiritual awareness and provides an important teaching opportunity

There is a true story about three children aged four to nine who decided to have a funeral for their recently deceased squirrel. They had a procession, carrying the corpse in a shoebox, the youngest bearing some withered daisies. The seven-year-old clasped an old dictionary in place of a prayer book because it had 'gold squirly writing on it'.

They closed their eyes while the eldest intoned, 'In the name of the Father, and of the Son and in-the-hole-he-goes.' With that the box lid was whisked off and the squirrel deftly shot into the prepared grave. The parents, who had to hide their amusement, admitted that the Holy Ghost had now taken on a whole new meaning for them!

Where do children learn about processions, solemnity, flowers on graves and special prayers to God? They view it on the TV news, see a hearse or drive past a cemetery. What they need is reinforcement for the parts they have right and amendment for those they are muddled about.

In the face of death, even a child with no religious upbringing will be confronted with religious words. 'Granny has gone to heaven' (as opposed to London or Margate) and 'Jesus came and took her.' In an interfaith school, teachers have a responsibility to address the child's spiritual understanding, by at least directing him or her to people who can give an explanation. Teachers can explain to children their own belief systems, pointing out that there are other beliefs and that these will be part of the child's future discovery.

In a school that is not markedly interfaith, it is easy to give facts about Jesus from the Christmas and Easter stories and to talk about heaven. Where other faiths are represented, their perspectives of death should be explored.

> In the face of death, even a child with no religious upbringing will be confronted with religious words

11

Concepts of death

Teachers have become much better in recent years at explaining the facts of life, so why not the facts of death, too?

Teachers have become much better in recent years at explaining the facts of life, so why not the facts of death, too?

The problem is, we adults don't know what we believe. But, unlike the younger children in our care, we know that death is irreversible. For them a lost toy can be found during a spring clean. A distant auntie comes to stay, then disappears, but still sends birthday cards. An empty guinea-pig cage may soon be filled again.

It is hard for a child under six to comprehend that dead means gone for ever. After all, TV baddies, such as in *Tom & Jerry* cartoons, sustain total mutilation yet live for next week's episode. Never in a TV cartoon are the dead collected up, buried and mourned, leaving the aching hurt that the child now experiences.

In the case of juniors, they may well have studied simple pumping systems and related these to the heart and blood supply. They will rightly question what happens when the heart stops. Death ensues. Many will know someone whose cat or dog has died and will have been told a variety of old wives' tales.

As they study history and read of kings being beheaded or Egyptians being mummified, they are ready for facts we might think are too gruesome for them. Their need to make sense of the facts of death provides a marvellous teaching opportunity.

Junior children want *facts.* Dead objects don't need food, water or care. They also decay. Children know this from having kept tadpoles in a jamjar or smelt the water in a vase of dead daffodils left in the classroom over half term. What they also need to know is, 'Does *everything* decay? And where does heaven (or reincarnation) fit into all this?'

Effects on the school

When a staff member or pupil dies, the whole school is affected. How should the children be told? Should the parents be informed by letter or should an announcement be made in assembly?

Each school will need to decide its own response. Indeed, governors are well advised to draw up a policy so that it is known to staff and in place before the need to implement it arises.

It is also important to consider when the collective grieving ritual is complete so that the school can return to normal. In fact, there is no 'normal' - there is simply a new state in which all have shared in the same hurt and that may well have deepened relationships in the school.

For children, the experience will have forced them to acknowledge that death isn't just reserved for old people. If a child has been killed crossing the road or died having a minor operation, it may well shake children's sense of security, causing them to to want to explore their own mortality.

In such a situation it is quite appropriate to have a class discussion with juniors on whether they want to be buried or cremated, or whether they would want their mountain bike given to a child who has nothing or just left for little brother to bash up.

> For children, the experience will have forced them to acknowledge that death isn't just reserved for old people

Death of a staff member

1. Reaction of adults

Teaching and ancillary staff will be shocked by the news, even if the person has been ill. We adults have an inbuilt resistance to accepting death, especially if it is someone our age or younger.

If it was a staff member you may be inclined to limit your involvement on the grounds that you don't want to get in the way of the immediate family. You will also try not to be shocked or sad - you have a class waiting to be taught, and the show must go on. Yet it's worth grasping the educational opportunity by involving the children.

How should we tell them? How much do they need to know? What if we burst into tears? These are some of the natural misgivings flying around the staffroom.

Some thought must also be given to the pupils directly affected. The replacement staff member - supply teacher, caretaker or dinner lady - may be treated with anger. Anger is a natural outworking of grief. It takes a lot for the replacement person to acknowledge with the children that they would rather have their old teacher back, but it is worth it.

It is often easier to tell the children all together. This task probably falls to the headteacher, but the head may appreciate being bailed out by another staff member explaining the contingency arrangements.

Adults in the school need to understand that other staff members are hurting and probably fearful of showing it to colleagues. A few hugs and spare tissues can be very meaningful. Tears, anger, disbelief and fear are natural accompaniments to grief, but they don't sit lightly on the shoulders of staff.

Don't be afraid to show pupils that adults as well as children can hurt

It is important that, rather than trying to carry on as if nothing has happened, the teacher acknowledges that the school family is hurting. Don't be afraid to show pupils that adults as well as children can hurt.

Where ancillary staff come across children who have been particularly affected by the death, they should try to encourage them to talk. A friendly arm and a gentle, 'You must be missing Miss Thomsett,' can give permission to open up the subject; the flow of tears is very valuable.

2. Reaction of pupils

Initially, especially with younger children, there may not be a pronounced reaction to a death. Infants may not see its relevance to them, but over the ensuing days they may feel the effect that its impact has on other pupils. At this age they are essentially selfish. They may cry not so much because Mrs Smith has died but because they had lent her their special Japanese doll in traditional costume, and they fear that it won't be returned.

Older children need to be given permission to cry and an opportunity to make their own unique contribution

Those children directly affected may ask penetrating questions, but then show normal behaviour for a while. This is often misconstrued as the children having got over the death quickly or not really caring. The fact is that in a normal day the child is only aware of the school caretaker or Mrs Smith intermittently whereas adults are preoccupied with the loss and unable to get on with their daily routine.

Older children need to be given permission to cry and an opportunity to make their own unique contribution. Some may want to write poems or make cards or flower arrangements. Others will be prepared to read at the funeral or in class. Decide what

16

will be done individually and what collectively, but make sure each contribution is appropriate.

Death of a pupil

Where a pupil dies, the affected class will grieve much longer than the rest of the school. Those who had a close friendship with the dead child will need some extra care.

> Where a pupil dies, the affected class will grieve much longer than the rest of the school

If the child had a specified workspace, leave a gap and occasionally refer to it. This gives permission for grief to continue in the hearts and minds of the children. The dead child made a contribution to the class and continues to be part of it because of his/her death. During the holidays will be the natural time to allow for movement of furniture and the space to be diminished as the class moves on in time.

Multiple loss in the school

Where several children and teachers die in one accident, staff, parents, pupils, governors, statutory agencies and the press all become entwined. Areas of responsibility need to be clear. Senior staff and governors may deal with outside agencies but they also have a duty to other staff, children and parents. Information needs to be verified before being formally given.

Parts of the school may be set aside where grieving and sharing can take place, preferably with a coffee machine and counsellors on hand.

Up to at least a week after the funerals, each day could combine normal working, time out for grieving, a formal remembrance and information time. Pupils will be grateful for a routine, even though they are preoccupied. They may want to cry, express their pain in drawings or go to the 'set apart' area. They will also need to know they won't be told off for not completing their work.

There is a delicate balance between reacting to the shock and moving on. The most vulernable are the junior members of staff, who are dealing directly with the children's questions and pain.

The anxiety-cum-relief of survivors and their relatives is a real issue that needs talking through. Grieving parents may form support groups, while parents of survivors may feel isolated in their guilt. The school could offer a coffee evening to all parents to discuss how the bereavement is being dealt with. This could be coupled with planning a memorial. It would serve to bring bereaved and survivor parents face to face in controlled circumstances.

A coffee evening would serve to bring bereaved and survivor parents face to face

How the school responds

1. Collectively

The response to a death could be minimal, with just a staff member attending the funeral. On the other hand, it could involve working with the children to write a letter of condolence, making cards and prayers, or even taking part in the funeral service. In the latter case, the family needs to be consulted because the combination of children and death is itself very tear-jerking.

Generally, other than a loss in the immediate family, it is best for children to be given the choice about attending the funeral service. If children attend, having some parent helpers can relieve the stress on bereaved teachers. If it is a child who has died, staff need to be prepared for the extra shock of seeing a small coffin.

> Naturally, many children attending the funeral will cry, but they can also be encouraged to say goodbye and to commit the person into God's care

Children attending a funeral should be told clearly what will happen. Naturally, many will cry, but they can also be encouraged to say goodbye and to commit the person into God's care.

On returning to school they can do a special activity and be given a drink and biscuit as a treat. This allows those affected to come back out of their sadness and those not so affected to let rip after the solemnity of the funeral.

Those who didn't attend can be involved in making a flower arrangement or picture to go into each classroom or the headteacher's office.

In these ways the school collectively acknowledges the death, admits that they are all in some way affected, and uses a variety of ways for showing their sorrow and care. A suitable class outing could be to go to the cemetery a few days later and see the flowers. This could be combined with a learning project, such as the kind of trees growing there or the different types of writing on the headstones.

2. Helping individuals

Some children may be more deeply affected than others by the death of a staff member or pupil. Try to determine why this is. A family member in hospital may have died recently. They may feel somehow responsible yet confused that their action or neglect has caused this degree of upset in the school.

Help them to explore their feelings and raise questions. They may be angry that classmates seem unaffected. Acknowledge this legitimate feeling. Allow for their preoccupation and give them short tasks that fit their concentration span. Reinforce their security where you can.

It is easier for someone with a confused or frightened mind to work with a couple of friends on practical things than to deal with cognitive matters at the same speed as the rest of the class. Use the different levels of reaction to teach the class about depths of relationships. Encourage them to express friendship and concern for each other. Don't allow the fantasy that the dead person was perfect.

Use the different levels of reaction to a death to teach the class about depths of relationships

Case study

You are informed that seven-year-old Matthew is staying with Grandma while Mum is in hospital. Three days later you learn that mum has died. Who needs to know? Should the children be told? If so, should it be just the class or the whole school?

A good way is for the class teacher to visit the father at home to discuss how best to handle Matthew's return. Subject to the parent's wishes, it is useful to tell Matthew's class while he is away and to make a card to send him.

All staff, including the school secretary and caretaker, need to know the situation so they can express condolences to Matthew on his return. On the first few days back it may be helpful to involve him with adults and just one or two classmates. He will appreciate being special - but not singled out, which is different.

Help the class receive Matthew on his first day back. Link his return with other projects, such as the weather. 'Yesterday was wet and windy, and today the sun's out. Yesterday was a nasty day for Matthew. Do you want to tell us what happened?' This may free him to talk about his mum's funeral or some other aspect. Make sure you have your facts right, though.

Use the opportunity to tell the class that Matthew will feel sad for a long time because he will be missing his mum. Be especially sensitive if the death occurs around Mother's Day or Easter.

The bereaved child may experience mood swings of high excitement and total withdrawal

1. Effects on adults

Other adults will tend to avoid Matthew in the same way they might avoid a bereaved neighbour. Encourage them instead to say how sorry they are and to ask about other relatives. It is helpful to reinforce for the child that it has really happened and other people know about it. If this causes him to cry, that may be another reason to give him a hug - something he needs. It helps him learn that tears are acceptable. He will soon return to the day's activities.

2. Effects on the child

a. Emotional

Matthew may experience mood swings of high excitement and total withdrawal. He may cry over small things and may display regressive behaviour - thumb sucking, rocking or wanting to be close to adults. He may be anxious at home time that those caring for him might forget him. Reassurance is the keynote here.

Be patient. Acknowledge that he is very sad and that his mum won't be coming back. He may ask for facts about heaven or how it feels to be dead. He may talk of running into the road or cutting himself. There is an objective fascination about death as well as a subjective loss and fear.

Acknowledge that he is very sad and that his mum won't be coming back

b. Educational

He will tend to lose ground in what he has recently learnt. His concentration span will be short and he will be easily distracted. His drawings and stories may have a predominance of death in them - a normal outworking of grief.

Make sure you correct any misinformation. If Grandma has told him Mum has turned into a star or is now an angel holding his hand as he crosses the road, should you countermand her fantasy? Children need concrete facts. Tell him what you believe and admit that Grandma may believe something else. Teach the whole class what stars are made of and point out that tangible adults' hands need to be held when crossing the road.

Long term, Matthew may fall behind while he adjusts to the social changes at home. He will thrive on encouragement at quite small progress and he will need to know that it takes a long time to get over a major death.

c. Behavioural

He may well attention-seek. Try to ignore the bad and involve him in helping other children and adults. He needs to discover that his mum's death wasn't his fault. Sadly, children are often told, 'You'll be the death of me,' or, 'I'll kill you if you say that again.' It's not surprising that children equate death with something wrong they have done. They might wish the substitute carer dead so their real mum will return, and they might try to make it happen by behaving badly.

A few hugs and admitting, 'I know you're unhappy,' are helpful. Eventually he may settle into a routine but slip back into grief at holiday times or religious festivals. If he clings to you as a surrogate mother, share him out with other adults. He may show aggression to others. Help him to realise the anger inside him and to redirect it in sport or other constructive activities rather than thumping his classmates.

Older children

Older children stand more of a chance of being included in family discussions and funeral plans.

When a death occurs, children will often find some 'wrong' they did to the deceased and assume that this caused the death. The school has an important role to play here in explaining that death is caused by something pretty big and not by what a small child may or may not have done.

24

Fantasy is far more frightening than reality. Children who are told they can't see their dead relative or go to the funeral may well find their minds running off into the realm of the horror videos. If a child in your class has been fortunate enough to view a body or attend a funeral, get the child to discuss this. How did it feel? What did they understand was happening? Was there anything left unsaid or undone? Such discussion provides an opportunity to correct misinformation.

One family stopped in the middle of burying the ashes of a one-year-old because his 10-year-old sister insisted on writing a poem to be buried under the rose tree among the ashes. It seemed almost farcical when the girl twice ran into the garden to ask how to spell 'remembered' and what rhymed with 'everlasting'. But the family waited patiently. Later, the girl's teacher would be able to use the opportunity to have classroom discussion about the way sadness is expressed in humans.

It is imperative that junior children be given the choice of whether or not to go to the funeral. If they prefer to come to school, they may need space at the time of the funeral to do their own joining in - perhaps reading quietly or going to the sick room. If an adult could explain that funerals generally have a few prayers and two hymns, and that the service usually lasts no more than 15 minutes, that will be useful information they may not get elsewhere.

In the early weeks children's academic work

will suffer. This should be acknowledged and the children encouraged to do their best. Their concentration span is diminished and it may be possible to break up the time with visits to the library or other diversions. Strong, irrational outbursts will be experienced, and it is helpful to tell the children affected that they will find themselves short-tempered. Running an errand or giving children a chance to explain how they feel can be a help.

For adults, bereavement takes two to three years. Children will oscillate between getting on with the here and now and lapsing into periods of mourning. There may be changes of family circumstances for a bereaved child and this will affect behaviour. In such circumstances school provides possibly the greatest stability the child has. Such a child will need firm, consistent handling and acknowledgement that you understand the churned-up feelings.

Children sometimes become preoccupied with death, even when there is no apparent bereavement. When talking to parents, ask if there has been a significant loss in the family or neighbourhood. If the death of a distant relative or neighbour coincides with the child's interest in death, its relevance can be important.

Children often have a deep attachment to a family pet and can be devastated at the death of a cat or dog, especially if it has lived in the family for as long as the child. Adults may dismiss grief over animals as

Adults may dismiss grief over animals as silly and sentimental, leaving the child feeling that mourning is inappropriate. Please assure them that it is not

26

silly and sentimental, leaving the child feeling that mourning is inappropriate. Please assure them that it is not.

Effects on the home

Death in a family causes major disruption for many months. Children tend to be left to their own devices and may either withdraw or rebel. Having lost one parent it is natural to fear they will lose the second just as rapidly. Others might be spoilt where adults try to compensate them for the loss.

As a staff member you may be asked if children should see the body or attend the funeral. Generally, children should be offered a choice, having had some explanation of what will happen. It is part of their education and a vital part of saying goodbye. Children need to see their parents grieving. This gives the children permission to grieve and shows them that adults have the same feelings.

The key is not to divert children from grief but to acknowledge its validity and encourage them that one day they won't feel as sad as they do now

The family may get anxious if the child's grief extends over several weeks. It is helpful to let them know that for the first year or two there will be repeated times of sadness, especially at birthdays and Christmas. The key is not to divert children from grief but to acknowledge its validity and encourage them that one day they won't feel as sad as they do now.

The teacher is frequently seen by the parent as a wise counsellor. Looking at any situation from a different perspective is valuable, but try to understand the parent's hurt, too. Months after the death parents may despair at a PTA or parent's evening about the child's behavioural or educational decline. They may not be aware that the bereavement is still taking its toll.

At this stage the school could recommend a counsellor or some helpful books to the parent.

Spiritual issues

Spiritual issues are governed by the teacher's perspective and by the family's background. Some teachers, for instance, will have a strong belief system which says that God has given humanity the choice of spending eternity with him or in hell without him. That choice, they contend, is held until the very last moments of life. Jesus said to the thief on the cross, 'Today you will be with me in paradise.'

Other teachers will share with the children their own doubts about this mystery and teach that there are a number of different beliefs held, especially in a multicultural school. Juniors have inquisitive minds and may well be keen to conduct a mini-survey of all the adults in the school or some members of their family to discover what others believe and so begin to discover their own belief system.

Spiritual issues are governed by the teacher's perspective and by the family's background

Juniors can be taught that most religions believe that there is a part of us that lives on after death but which takes different forms. The most tangible example is the autumn leaf which, having died and fallen to the ground, is transformed into compost to enable the tree to go on living.

Generally in the UK, the church only features at baptism, marriage and death. If children are bombarded by stories about God wanting the dead person in heaven, they will feel that God is uncaring. Heaven becomes a place where everyone 'falls asleep'. Help children to understand that death is not falling asleep.

It was the drunk driver, not God, who ran into daddy and killed him. God cares very much that everyone is hurting and sends people to act as his helpers and comforters.

Jesus promises, 'I will never leave you or forsake you.' That is often a very real security for children.

Juniors can be taught that most religions believe that there is a part of us that lives on after death but which takes different forms

Summary

Our society is afraid of death and tends to push it away. Yet grief needs expressing in order to be understood. Young children live more in the present than adults do, and they seem to get over a death more quickly. Periodically, though, they will have times of grieving.

> **Teaching on death and dying should be an important part of the school curriculum**

Teaching on death and dying should be an important part of the school curriculum. Twenty years ago schools were inviting the district nurse in to show how a nappy was changed. Today, if a staff member has a baby she is asked to bring her baby back as a teaching aid and may well feel able to breastfeed the infant in the children's presence as part of their learning.

We have succeeded in teaching the facts of life. Let us now begin to teach the facts of death so that in a generation or two our society will be more informed and more healthy.

Helpful books and publications

For children

3 to 6 years
Gran's Grave, Wendy Green, Lion Publishing, 1989
My Book About . . . , St Christopher's Hospice, 1989

7 to 11 years
Waterbugs and Dragonflies, Doris Stickney, Mowbray, 1982
Badger's Parting Gift, Susan Varley, Collins, 1994
Far Side of the Shadow, Peggy Burns, Harvestime, 1987
Emma Says Goodbye, Carolyn Nystrom, Lion Publishing, 1994

Special needs
When Mum Died, Sheila Hollins & Lester Sireling, Silent, 1989
When Dad Died, Sheila Hollins & Lester Sireling, Silent, 1989

Professional

Grief in Children, Atle Dyregrove, Kingsley, 1990
An invaluable book with passages giving advice to schools.

Losing a Child, Elaine Storkey, Lion Publishing, 1989
A pocket book full of understanding.

Good Grief, Barbara Ward and Associates, Kingsley, 1987
Exceptionally good. Includes class projects, worksheets and
advice on school grief.

Helping Children Cope with Grief, Rosemary Wells, Sheldon
Press, 1992
Practical book for adults who deal with children after a family
death.

General

Living Through Grief, Harold Bauman, Lion Publishing, 1987
A pocket book offering real direction and comfort.

Bereavement: A Shared Experience, Helen Alexander, Lion Publishing, 1993
A compilation of people's experiences, reactions and feelings, offering insight, direction and empathy.

A Grief Observed, C.S. Lewis, Faber & Faber, 1976.

All in the End is Harvest: An anthology for those who grieve, Ed: Agnes Whitaker, Darton, Longman & Todd, 1985.
Useful snippets for teachers wanting to help pupils compile a reading for a funeral.

Coping with Loss, R. Lascelles, Pepar, 1986.
Sets out the stages of the grieving process that many people experience.

Most of the above books can be obtained from:

Family Reading Centre Ltd
126 Sutherland Avenue
Biggin Hill
Kent TN16 3HJ
Telephone: 0959-575172   Fax: 0959-576445